Also by Lee Cooper
FUN WITH SPANISH

By Lee Cooper and Clifton McIntosh
FUN WITH FRENCH

FUN WITH ITALIAN

FUN WITH

ITALIAN

by Lee Cooper
Marion Greene
Lia Beretta

Illustrated by Ann Atene

LITTLE, BROWN
AND COMPANY
Boston   Toronto

Published simultaneously in Canada
by Little, Brown & Company (Canada) Limited

PRINTED IN THE UNITED STATES OF AMERICA

INDICE

To Coralynn Cooper,
Meg Greene and Ugo Beretta

FUN WITH ITALIAN

IL CIRCO

Arriva il circo.

Passa la banda con la musica.

Passano molti carri e animali.

Gina e Giovanni vanno al circo!

That was Gina and Giovanni.

They speak Italian.

Some of the Italian words look so familiar that you already know exactly what they mean. If you don't understand a word, look it up in the vocabulary in the back of this book.

But how do you *pronounce* these words? That's easy, too. Just follow Gina and Giovanni to this gay Italian circus.

Here's your ticket!

BIGLIETTI

"Ah!"

When the letter *a* appears, everyone always says "Ah."

la (lah): the

balla (BAHL-lah): he, she dances

canta (KAHN-tah): he, she sings

la gatta (GAHT-tah): cat

salta (SAHL-tah): he, she jumps over

la casa (KAH-sah): house

La gatta balla.
La gatta canta.
La gatta salta.
La gatta salta la casa.

"Hey!"

The letter *e* performs on the tight wire and sounds like the *e* in *hey*.

But sometimes *e* sounds like the *e* in *net*.

il serpente (sehr-PEHN-tay): serpent

nero (NAY-roh): black

è (eh): is

enorme (ay-NOR-may): enormous; huge

il cane (KAH-nay): dog

vede (VAY-day): he, she sees

teme (TAY-may): he, she fears

Il serpente è nero.
Il serpente è enorme.
Il cane vede il serpente.
Il cane teme il serpente.

"Ee!"

The letter *i* swings by the feet.

And that's the way *i* always sounds, like the *ee* in *feet*.

il (eel): the

il pinguino (peen-goo‿EE-noh): penguin

bianco (bee‿AHN-koh): white

addio (ahd-DEE-oh): good-by

grida (GREE-dah): he, she shouts

i birilli (bee-REEL-lee): bowling pins

Il pinguino è bianco e nero.
La palla è bianca e nera.
Il pinguino getta la palla.
La palla salta i birilli.
"Addio," grida il pinguino.

"Oh!"

The letter *o* swings on a rope and sounds like the *o* in *rope*.

But sometimes *o* sounds like the *o* in *top*.

l'orso (OHR-soh): bear

piccolo (PEEK-koh-loh): little

grosso (GROS-soh): large

non (nohn): not

la corda (KOHR-dah): rope

vola (VOH-lah): he, she flies

L'orso non è piccolo.
L'orso è grosso.
La corda vola.
L'orso vola.

"Oo!"

The letter *u* is going to jump into a sword-rimmed pool.

She always sounds like the *oo* in *pool*.

una (oo-nah): a; an

guarda (goo‿AHR-dah): he, she looks at

la cangura (kahn-GOO-rah): kangaroo

le punte (POON-tay): points

buffa (BOOF-fah): funny

vuole (voo‿o-lay): he, she wants

Guarda la cangura!
La cangura teme le punte.
La cangura non vuole saltare.
Una cangura è buffa.

C before *e* or *i* sounds like the *c* in *cheese*.

il ciuco (chee‿oo-koh): donkey

il cucciolo (koo-chee‿OH-loh): puppy

dice (DEE-chay): he, she says

ciao (chee‿AH-oh): hello; good-by

Il ciuco guarda il cucciolo.
"Ciao," dice il ciuco.
Il cucciolo teme il ciuco.
"Addio," dice il cucciolo.

Ch sounds like the *k* in *key*.

la chioccia (kee‿o-chee‿ah): mother-hen

la chiave (kee‿AH-vay): key

perchè (pehr-KAY): why; because

chi (kee): who

chiede (kee‿EH-day): he, she asks

chicchirichi (kee-kee-ree-KEE): cock-a-doodle-doo

La chioccia ha* una chiave.

Perchè ha una chiave?

Perchè vuole entrare in casa.

"Chi è in casa?" chiede la chioccia

"Chicchirichi," dice il gallo.

*Ha (has) is pronounced *ah* because the letter *h* in Italian is always silent.

G before *e* or *i* sounds like the g in *giraffe*.

buon giorno (boo͜on jee͜OHR-noh): good morning

mangiano (MAHN-jee͜ah-noh): they eat

il gelato (jay-LAH-toh): ice cream

la giraffa (jee-RAHF-fah): giraffe

piange (pee͜AHN-jay): he, she cries

"Buon giorno," dice Giovanni.

"Buon giorno," dice Gina.

Giovanni e Gina mangiano il gelato.

La giraffa vuole il gelato.

La giraffa piange perchè non ha il gelato.

Gh sounds like the g in *spaghetti*.

il ghiro (GHEE-roh): dormouse

gli spaghetti (spah-GHEHT-tee): spaghetti

lunghi (LOON-ghee): long

Il ghiro mangia spaghetti.
Gli spaghetti sono lunghi.
Il ghiro mangia molti spaghetti.
Il ghiro è una palla di spaghetti!

Gl sounds like the *ll* in *millions* of rabbits.

il pagliaccio (pah-lyee‿AH-chee‿oh): clown

il coniglio (koh-NEE-lyee‿oh): rabbit

egli (EH-lyee): he

la bottiglia (boht-TEE-lyee‿ah): bottle

meraviglioso (may-rah-vee-lyee‿OH-zoh): marvel-
    lous (sometimes *s* is pronounced *z*)

Il pagliaccio ha molti conigli.
Egli ha conigli bianchi e conigli neri.
I conigli sono in una bottiglia.
Meraviglioso!

The *gn* sounds like the *ny* in *canyon*.

la cicogna (chee-KOH-nyah): stork
sogna (SOH-nyah): he, she dreams
disegna (dee-SAY-nyah): he, she draws
magnifica (mah-NYEE-fee-kah): magnificent

La cicogna sogna una fotografia.
La fotografia è magnifica.
La cicogna disegna la fotografia.
È magnifica!

Qu sounds like the *qu* in *quiet*.

l'aquila (AH-koo‿ee-lah): eagle

cinque (CHEEN-koo‿ay): five

gli aquilotti (ah-koo‿ee-LOT-tee): eaglets

quattro (koo‿AHT-troh): four

quieto (koo‿ee‿EH-toh): quiet

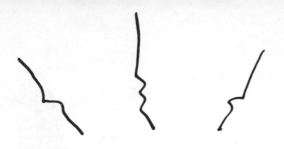

L'aquila ha cinque aquilotti.

Un aquilotto è piccolo.

Quattro aquilotti sono grossi.

L'aquila guarda i cinque aquilotti.

L'aquilotto piccolo è quieto.

Gli aquilotti grossi non sono quieti.

The *r* always rolls.

la zebra (DZAY-brah): zebra

sempre (SEHM-pray): always

rotola (RO-toh-lah): he, she rolls

il circo (CHEER-koh): circus

sorride (sohr-REE-day): he, she smiles

La zebra sempre rotola.
La zebra rotola nel circo.
Ella rotola, rotola, rotola.
La zebra sorride.

Sc before *e* or *i* sounds like the *sh* in *fish*. (Before *a, o,* or *u, sc* sounds like the *sk* in *skate*.)

il pesce (PAY-shay): fish

la vasca (VAH-skah): pool

la scatola (SKAH-toh-lah): box

discende (dee-SHAYN-day): he, she descends

scompare (skohm-PAH-ray): he, she disappears

Il pesce è in una vasca.
La scatola è in una vasca.
Il pesce salta la scatola.
Il pesce discende.
Il pesce scompare.

Z or *zz* usually sounds like the *ts* in *eats*. (Sometimes *z* or *zz* sounds like *dz*.)

il ragazzo (rah-GAHT-soh): boy

mezza (MEHD-zah): half

la pizza (PEET-sah): pizza pie

la mozzarella (mot-sah-REHL-lah): mozzarella cheese

la bellezza (behl-LAYT-sah): beauty

Il ragazzo mangia mezza pizza.
La pizza è con mozzarella.
La pizza è grossa.
La pizza è una bellezza.

IL SIGNORE e LA SIGNORA

"The book is HE."

"The house is SHE."

Doesn't it sound strange to refer to the book and the house as *he* and *she?* In Italian *every* object is a HE or a SHE.

For this reason, you may have noticed more than one word meaning *the*.

THE with HE Words

il (eel): the
(Before most singular HE words.)

il pinguino

i (ee): the
(Before most plural HE words beginning with a consonant.)

i pinguini

lo (loh): the
(Before singular HE words beginning with z, or s plus a consonant.)

lo scimpanzè

gli (lyee): the
(Before plural HE words beginning with a vowel, or z, or s plus a consonant.)

gli scimpanzè

THE with SHE Words

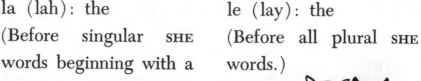

la (lah): the
(Before singular SHE
words beginning with a
consonant.)

le (lay): the
(Before all plural SHE
words.)

la gatta

le gatte

THE with HE or SHE Words

l': the
(Before singular HE or
SHE words beginning
with a vowel.

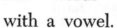

l'orso

l'aquila

Did you notice that most singular HE words ended with *o* and most singular SHE words ended with *a*?

Keep that in mind as you play this game of Tick-Tack-Toe with il signore and la signora.

First, draw a Tick-Tack-Toe diagram on a separate sheet of paper (do not write in the book).

If the word is a HE word, write *il* in the space having the same number; if the word is a SHE word, write *la*.

Il signore wants to win. Does he?

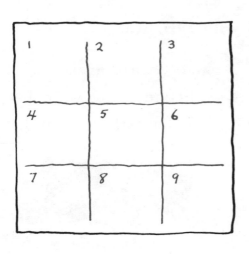

1. _____ palla
2. _____ circo
3. _____ cangura
4. _____ cucciolo
5. _____ casa
6. _____ ciuco
7. _____ pinguino
8. _____ ragazzo
9. _____ gatta

UN SIGNORE e UNA SIGNORA

A and *AN* with *HE* Words

uno (oo-noh): a; an
(Before a HE word beginning with *z*, or *s* plus a consonant.)

un (oon): a; an
(Before any other HE word.)

uno scoiattolo

un pappagallo

A and *AN* with *SHE* words

una (oo-nah): a; an
(Before a SHE word beginning with a consonant.)

un' (oon): a; an
(Before a SHE word beginning with a vowel.)

una chitarra

un'aquila

Will un signore or una signora win this game of
Tick-Tack-Toe?

Find out by drawing a Tick-Tack-Toe diagram on
a separate sheet of paper. Write *un* if the word is a
HE word and *una* if the word is a SHE word.

1. _____ scatola
2. _____ ghiro
3. _____ vasca
4. _____ coniglio
5. _____ gelato
6. _____ giraffa
7. _____ cicogna
8. _____ pagliaccio
9. _____ orso

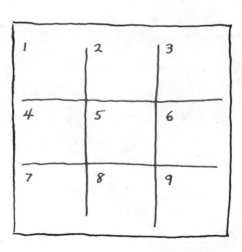

ATTRAZIONI DEL CIRCO

Il circo ha molte attrazioni:

i cani che ballano,

il pappagallo che canta,

il ciuco che suona la chitarra,

e scimmie,

scimmie,

scimmie,

e ancora scimmie!

IL RISTORANTE

Il circo ha una cangura che ha un ristorante.

"Buon giorno," dice la cangura.

"Buon giorno," dicono Gina e Giovanni, "come stai?"

Ristorante della Cangura

LISTA

Antipasto

Spaghetti   Ravioli

Bistecca

Insalata

Asparagi   Spinaci   Carote

Frutta

Animali di Cioccolato

Caffè   Latte   Limonata

"Sto bene, grazie," dice la cangura. "E tu come stai?"

"Io ho fame," dice Giovanni.

"Vuoi mangiare gli spaghetti?"

"No," dice Giovanni, "voglio mangiare un elefante, un leone, una giraffa, un'aquila e un orso."

"Tu hai molta fame," dice Gina, "ma io non ho molta fame. Io voglio mangiare solamente una piccola scimmia."

La cangura non capisce.

Ella guarda la lista.

"Sono sulla lista gli elefanti, i leoni, le giraffe, le aquile, gli orsi e le scimmie?" domanda la cangura.

"Sì," dice Giovanni.

"Sì," dice Gina.

La cangura guarda ancora la lista.

Poi ella capisce. Ella sorride.

Ella dà a Giovanni un elefante, un leone, una giraffa, un'aquila e un orso.

Ella dà a Gina una scimmia.

"Grazie, cangura," dice Giovanni.

"Grazie, cangura," dice Gina.

E essi mangiano gli animali di cioccolato.

I BUONI AMICI

NOUNS and ADJECTIVES are very good friends. They *always* agree.

If the noun is SHE singular, the adjective is SHE singular.

If the noun is HE singular, the adjective is HE singular.

la palla nera

il birillo nero

If the noun is SHE plural, the adjective is SHE plural.

If the noun is HE plural, the adjective is HE plural.

le palle nere

i birilli neri

If a singular noun or adjective ends with *e*, its plural ends with *i*.

Let's bowl!

Here's a game that's fun to play by yourself or with friends.

Write each of these words on a slip of paper: *palla, palle, birillo, birilli*. Put the four slips in one box. Write each of these words on a slip of paper: *nera, nere, nero, neri*. Put these slips in another box.

Draw one slip from each box. If the words "agree" (if both are plural HE, for example) the player scores (one point for singular words and two points for plural). Return each slip to its box after each drawing.

When a player makes a strike he receives *two* extra draws. (A "strike" means that the player has scored ten points in only five draws.)

When a player makes a spare he receives *one* extra draw. (A "spare" means that the player has scored ten points in only six draws.)

If more than one person plays, take turns drawing.

After ten draws by each player (not counting extra draws for strikes and spares), total the scores. The player who has the highest score is the winner.

IL PINGUINO

Il pinguino Pogo ha un'ombra.

Quando c'è il sole, l'ombra è sempre con Pogo.

Ma quando il sole scompare dietro una nuvola, anche l'ombra di Pogo scompare.

L'ombra di Pogo imita Pogo.

Pogo pattina sul ghiaccio.

L'ombra di Pogo pattina sul ghiaccio.

Pogo fa un otto.
L'ombra di Pogo fa un
otto.

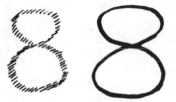

Pogo fa un quadrato.
L'ombra di Pogo fa un
quadrato.

Pogo fa un triangolo.
L'ombra di Pogo fa un
triangolo.

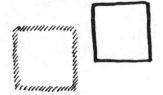

Pogo fa un rettangolo.
L'ombra di Pogo fa un
rettangolo.

Pogo e la sua ombra sanno disegnare:

una bambina,

un bambino,

un indiano.

Essi leggono.

Essi scrivono.

Essi cantano.

Ma un giorno l'ombra di Pogo è triste.

L'ombra sa fare tutto quello che sa fare Pogo, ma non sa fare quello che Pogo non sa fare.

"Voglio fare qualche cosa che tu non sai fare," dice l'ombra di Pogo.

Pogo fa i cerchi.

L'ombra di Pogo fa i cerchi.

L'ombra di Pogo vuole fare più cerchi di Pogo.

Pogo fa cerchi,

cerchi,

cerchi,

e ancora cerchi!

Pogo fa dieci, venti, trenta cerchi.

Pogo fa quaranta, cinquanta, sessanta cerchi.

Pogo fa settanta, ottanta, novanta cerchi.

Pogo fa cento cerchi.

L'ombra di Pogo fa cento cerchi.

L'ombra non sa fare più cerchi di Pogo.

L'ombra è molto triste.

Poi il sole va dietro una nuvola.

L'ombra di Pogo scompare.

Poi il sole riappare.

E l'ombra di Pogo riappare.

L'ombra è ancora triste.

"Voglio fare qualche cosa che tu non sai fare," dice l'ombra a Pogo.

"Ma tu sai fare qualche cosa che io non so fare," dice Pogo. "Sai scomparire!"

gennaio	febbraio	marzo	aprile
maggio	giugno	luglio	agosto
settembre	ottobre	novembre	dicembre

IL CALENDARIO

Gina guarda il calendario.

"Quale è il tuo mese preferito, Giovanni?" domanda Gina. "È gennaio, febbraio o marzo?"

"No," dice Giovanni.

"È aprile, maggio o giugno?"

"No."

"È luglio, agosto o settembre?"

"No."

"È ottobre, novembre o dicembre?"

"No."

"E allora quale è il tuo mese preferito?"

"È il mese quando il circo viene in città!" risponde Giovanni.

IL PAPPAGALLO

Ecco il pappagallo Cocò.
Egli è molto intelligente.
È il pappagallo più intelligente del mondo!
"Sa leggere l'ora?" domanda Gina.
"Naturalmente," dice Giovanni. "È molto intel-
ligente."
Gina muove le lancette dell'orologio.

        Ora è l'una.

Ma Cocò non dice niente.

Gina muove ancora le lancette.

        Ora sono le nove e quindici.

        Ora sono le dieci.

        Ora sono le undici e trenta.

Ma Cocò ancora non dice niente.

Gina muove ancora una volta le lancette.

Ora sono le dodici.

Allora Cocò dice:

"Cocò vuole un biscotto."

Giovanni sorride e dice:

"Non è intelligente Cocò? Egli sa che le dodici è l'ora di mangiare!"

I CUCCIOLI

Titta è un cane.

Titta è un cane parlante.

Ella ha due cuccioli.

Un giorno domanda:

"Dove sono i miei cuccioli?"

I cuccioli non ci sono.

È l'una.

Titta non trova Bibì.

Sono le due.

E Titta non trova Bibò.

Sono le tre.

Titta non trova Bibì e Bibò.

Sono le quattro.

I suoi cuccioli non ci sono più.

Sono le cinque.

Ora Titta piange.

"Dove sono i miei cuccioli?" domanda Titta a Gina.
"Come si chiamano i tuoi cuccioli?"
"Si chiamano Bibì e Bibò," dice la povera mamma.
Poi mette la testa su una scatola e piange.
"Cerchiamo i cuccioli," dice Giovanni.

Sono le sei.
Gina e Giovanni domandano
alla grassona del circo:
"Hai visto Bibì e Bibò?"
"No," risponde la grassona.

Poi domandano allo smilzo:
"Hai visto Bibì e Bibò?"
"No," dice lo smilzo.

Anche alla donna barbuta
domandano:
"Hai visto Bibì e Bibò?"
"No," dice la donna barbuta.

Sono le sette.

Gina e Giovanni guardano fra gli animali:

il serpente

la zebra

l'ippopotamo

il cammello

Ma non trovano Bibì e Bibò.

Sono le otto.

Gina e Giovanni guardano per la città.

Ma non trovano Bibì e Bibò.

Sono le nove.

Gina e Giovanni guardano qui, guardano là.

Guardano

nel Colosseo,

in una gondola,

nella Torre Pendente di Pisa.

Ma non trovano Bibì e Bibò.

Sono le dieci.

Gina e Giovanni ritornano al circo.

Titta piange ancora.

Ha ancora la testa sulla scatola.

Titta solleva la testa.

"Dove sono i miei cuccioli?" domanda Titta.

"Non sono in città," dice Giovanni. "Non sono nel Colosseo o nella gondola o sulla Torre Pendente."

"Noi non sappiamo dove sono," dice Gina.

Poi la scatola salta.

"Guarda la scatola!" grida Giovanni.

La scatola dice: "Bù, bù."

Giovanni ha paura.

Ma Titta solleva la scatola.

Vede Bibì, poi vede Bibò.

I cuccioli sono sotto la scatola!

Bibì e Bibò dicono:

"Anche noi vogliamo vedere il Colosseo, la gondola e la Torre Pendente di Pisa. La prossima volta che cercate Bibì e Bibò, vogliamo venire con voi!"

IL CIUCO

Questo è Tonio.

Tonio è un ciuco.

Tonio sta sempre seduto.

Ma egli vuole essere coraggioso come il resto della sua famiglia.

Sua madre sa pilotare un aeroplano.

Ella è molto coraggiosa.

Suo padre sa andare in bicicletta.

Egli è molto coraggioso.

Suo fratello e sua sorella vanno sull'altalena.

Sua sorella è in alto.

Suo fratello è in basso.

Essi sono molto coraggiosi.

Anche Tonio vuole essere coraggioso.

Ma egli sta sempre seduto . . .

. . . con la testa nella bocca del leone!

IL MAGO

Gina legge un cartello.
Il cartello dice:

Colpite i birilli!
Vincete i conigli!

"Vuoi vincere i conigli?" domanda Gina.

"No," dice Giovanni. "Mio zio Marco mi dà i conigli. Egli è un mago e ha molti conigli."

"Io voglio sette conigli," dice Gina. "Voglio chiamare i conigli come i sette giorni della settimana."

Ella getta una palla.

Ella colpisce un birillo.

Ella vince un grosso coniglio.

Ella mette il coniglio nel cappello.

Ella getta un'altra palla.

Ma ella non vince un altro coniglio.

Ella getta una, due, tre, quattro, cinque, sei, sette palle.

Ma ella vince solamente un coniglio.

"Voglio sette conigli," dice Gina.

"Mio zio Marco ha molti conigli," dice Giovanni. "Ora scrivo una lettera a mio zio Marco."

E Giovanni scrive questa lettera:

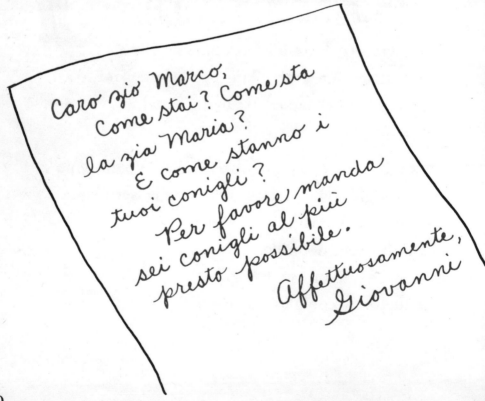

Caro zio Marco,
Come stai? Come sta
la zia Maria?
E come stanno i
tuoi conigli?
Per favore manda
sei conigli al più
presto possibile.
Affettuosamente,
Giovanni

E ora Gina grida:

"Il mio cappello è pesante. Il mio cappello è molto pesante."

Gina guarda nel cappello.

Anche Giovanni guarda nel cappello.

Essi vedono un grosso coniglio e uno, due, tre, quattro, cinque, sei piccoli conigli.

"Ora ho sette conigli," dice Gina. "I miei conigli si chiamano Lunedì, Martedì, Mercoledì, Giovedì, Venerdì, Sabato e Domenica."

Giovanni guarda la lettera che ha scritto e dice:

"Mio zio è un grande mago, non è vero?"

E Giovanni scrive alla fine della lettera:

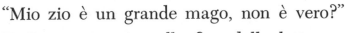

TOMBOLA

Everyone at the circus plays *tombola.*

Write on separate slips of paper the Italian words found below. Fold the papers and shake them in a box. Then cover this page so that only the opposite page shows.

1. il circo	2. la scatola	3. a palla
4. la chiave	5. la casa	6. il cane
7. l'orso	8. il serpente	9. la bottiglia

Now take a slip of paper from the box, read the Italian word, and place the paper in the square below that pictures this Italian word. Continue until you have placed three slips of paper in a row.

Then say, "Tombola!"

1.	2.	3.
4.	5.	6.
7.	8.	9.

IL PAGLIACCIO

Figaro è un pagliaccio.
Figaro ha una faccia buffa.
Ha gli occhi grandi.
Ha il naso rosso.
Ha la bocca bianca.
E ha le orecchie molto lunghe!

Figaro ha il cappello bianco.

Ha la camicia rossa.

Ha il pantaloni bianchi e rossi.

E ha le scarpe molto, molto l

u
n
g
h
e!

Figaro sa ballare con le sue lunghe scarpe.

Egli sa giocare al calcio con le sue lunghe scarpe.

Ma Figaro non sa salire le scale con le sue lunghe
scarpe.

E allora . . .

mani!

le

con

sale

egli

I PALLONI

"Quanto costa un pallone?" domanda Giovanni.

L'uomo risponde:

"Un pallone costa una lira."

"Quanto costano due palloni?"

"Due palloni costano due lire."

Giovanni conta il suo denaro.

Egli ha venti lire.

L'uomo conta i suoi palloni.

Egli ha venti palloni.

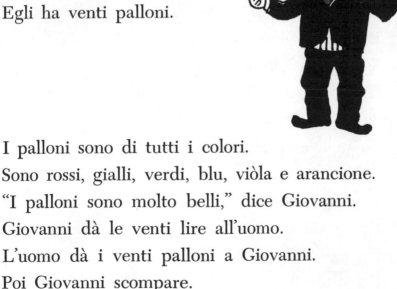

I palloni sono di tutti i colori.

Sono rossi, gialli, verdi, blu, viòla e arancione.

"I palloni sono molto belli," dice Giovanni.

Giovanni dà le venti lire all'uomo.

L'uomo dà i venti palloni a Giovanni.

Poi Giovanni scompare.

Dov'è Giovanni?

Egli sale su, su, su.

Scompare nelle nuvole.

"Aiuto!" grida. "I palloni mi portano nelle nuvole.
Aiuto!"

Le nuvole dicono:

"Aiuto! Aiuto!"

Il pappagallo Cocò guarda su.

Egli vede Giovanni.

Poi egli vede le nuvole.

Il pappagallo vola su per aiutare Giovanni.

"Per favore, aiuto!" grida Giovanni.

Cocò becca un pallone:

"Pum!"

Giovanni discende un poco.

Cocò becca un altro pallone, poi un altro e poi un altro.

I palloni scoppiano:

"Pum, pum, pum!"

Giovanni discende giù, giù.

Cocò becca tutti i palloni.

Tutti i palloni scoppiano.

Giovanni ora è in terra.

"Grazie," dice a Cocò.

Poi guarda le nuvole.

"Grazie anche a voi," dice.

E le nuvole in coro rispondono:

IL GIOCOLIERE

Gina vede una capra.

La capra è un giocoliere.

Il giocoliere fa girare un libro, una matita e una penna.

Poi prende una sedia.

Ora il giocoliere fa girare un libro, una matita, una penna e una sedia.

Poi prende un tavolo.

Ora il giocoliere fa girare un libro, una matita, una penna, una sedia e un tavolo.

"Guarda il giocoliere," dice Gina.

Ma Giovanni guarda la televisione.

Guarda il suo programma preferito, un film di cow-boys.

I cow-boys inseguono gli indiani.

Giovanni non vede il giocoliere.

La capra prende anche un divano.

Ora fa girare il libro, la matita, la penna, la sedia, il tavolo e il divano.

"Guarda," grida Gina, "il giocoliere fa girare tutto."

Ma Giovanni guarda ancora la televisione.

Ora gli indiani inseguono i cow-boys.

Ma ecco la capra prende la televisione.

Giovanni continua a guardare il film.

La televisione gira, gira, gira.

Poi la capra prende *Giovanni!*

E Giovanni gira, gira, gira.

Gira con la televisione.

E continua a guardare i cow-boys e gli indiani.

"Che programma interessante!" esclama Giovanni.

I cow-boys non inseguono più gli indiani.

Gli indiani non inseguono più i cow-boys.

La capra mette giù il libro, la matita e la penna.

Poi mette giù la sedia, il tavolo e il divano.

Alla fine mette giù Giovanni e la televisione.

Il programma finisce.

I cow-boys e gli indiani sono ora amici.

"Che programma interessante," dice Giovanni. "Mamma mia! Voglio fare anche io qualche cosa di interessante!"

LA MONETA

Oggi è il compleanno di Dumbo.

Dumbo ha cento anni.

Ma Dumbo è triste.

Il circo ora lascia l'Italia e Dumbo non vuole partire.

Dumbo è molto triste.

Tutti vogliono fare felice Dumbo.

La banda suona "Buon compleanno a te."

Tutti cantano:

"Buon compleanno a te,

Buon compleanno a te,

Buon compleanno, caro Dumbo,

Buon compleanno a te."

I cuccioli ballano
intorno a Dumbo.

Il pinguino pattina
davanti a Dumbo.

La cangura porta a Dumbo una torta.

La torta è molto, molto, molto grossa.

La torta ha cento candele.

Dumbo guarda la torta.

"Grazie," dice Dumbo alla cangura.

Ma Dumbo è ancora triste.

Dumbo non vuole lasciare l'Italia.

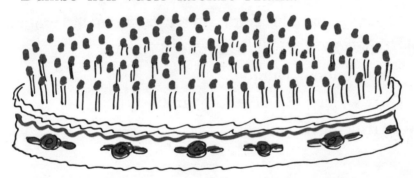

La capra fa girare i regali davanti a Dumbo.

Fa girare regali piccoli e grandi, regali lunghi e corti.

Fa girare regali rossi, arancione, blu, verdi, viòla e gialli.

Gina e Giovanni vogliono fare un regalo a Dumbo.

Vogliono dare un regalo a Dumbo perchè egli è triste.

Gina e Giovanni hanno un'idea.

Essi danno a Dumbo una moneta.

"Questa moneta è per la fontana di Trevi," dicono.

Dumbo sorride perchè capisce.

Dumbo getta la moneta nella fontana di Trevi.

Ora Dumbo è felice.

Egli sa che chi getta una moneta nella fontana di Trevi ritorna nella capitale d'Italia.

"Arrivederci, Dumbo."

"Arrivederci, Gina e Giovanni."

"Arrivederci, amici!"

IL CIRCOLO ITALIANO

This is not the end of your fun with Italian. It is just the beginning. Because now that you and your friends have read this book, you can organize an Italian Club.

Perhaps you'd like to name it *Il Circolo Italiano*. The first club business is to elect officers:

Ragazzi	*Ragazze*
Il Presidente	La Presidentessa
Il Vice-Presidente	La Vice-Presidentessa
Il Segretario	La Segretaria
Il Tesoriere	La Tesoriera

Find out the Italian names for all members and use these names during meetings.

Perhaps they will be listed on the following pages.

Adele (ah-DEH-lay): Adela

Agnese (ah-NYEH-say): Agnes

Alice (ah-LEE-chay): Alice

Amata (ah-MAH-tah: Amy

Anna (AHN-nah): Anne

Bianca (bee‿AHN-kah): Blanche

Carla (KAHR-lah): Charlotte

Carolina (kah-roh-LEE-nah): Caroline

Caterina (kah-tay-REE-nah): Catherine

Cinzia (CHEENT-see‿ah): Cynthia

Costanza (koh-STAHNT-sah): Constance

Cristina (kree-STEE-nah): Christine

Dorotea (doh-roh-TEH-ah): Dorothy

Edda (EHD-dah): Edith

Elena (EH-lay-nah): Helen

Elisabetta (ay-lee-zah-BEHT-tah): Elizabeth

Elisa (ay-LEE-zah): Elsie

Emilia (ay-MEE-lee‿ah): Emily

Enrichetta (ehn-ree-KEHT-tah): Harriet

Ester (EH-stayr): Esther

Fiorenza (fee‿oh-REHNT-sah): Florence

Franca (FRAHN-kah): Frances

Giovanna (jee‿oh-VAHN-nah): Joan

Giulia (jee‿oo-lee‿ah): Julia

Grazia (GRAHT-see‿ah): Grace

Isabella (ee-zah-BEHL-lah): Isabel

Lia (LEE-ah): Leah

Lidia (LEE-dee‿ah): Lydia

Lucia (loo-CHEE‿ah): Lucy

Luisa (loo‿EE-zah): Louise

Margherita (mahr-gay-REE-tah): Margaret

Maria (mah-REE‿ah): Mary

Marisa (mah-REE-za): Mary Lou

Marta (MAHR-tah): Martha

Nina (NEE-nah): Jenny

Patrizia (pah-TREET-see‿ah): Patricia

Paola (PAH‿oh-lah): Paula

Rita (REE-tah): Peggy

Sara (SAH-rah): Sarah

Susanna (soo-ZAHN-nah): Susan

Teresa (tay-REH-zah): Theresa

Vittoria (veet-TO-ree‿ah): Victoria

RAGAZZI

Alberto (ahl-BEHR-toh): Albert

Alfredo (ahl-FREH-doh): Alfred

Andrea (ahn-DREH‿ah): Andrew

Antonio (ahn-TO-nee‿oh): Anthony

Arnaldo (ahr-NAHL-doh): Arnold

Arturo (ahr-TOO-roh): Arthur

Beniamino (bay-nee‿ah-MEE-noh): Benjamin

Beppe (BEHP-pay): Joe

Bernardo (bayr-NAHR-doh): Bernard

Carlo (KAHR-loh): Charles

Cecco (CHAYK-koh): Frank

Cristoforo (kree-STO-foh-roh): Christopher

Davide (DAH-vee-day): David

Edoardo (ay-doh‿AHR-doh): Edward

Enrico (ayn-REE-koh): Henry

Erberto (ayr-BEHR-toh): Herbert

Ermanno (ayr-MAHN-noh): Herman

Ernesto (ayr-NEH-stoh): Ernest

Eugenio (ay‿oo-JEH-nee‿oh): Eugene

Francesco (frahn-CHAY-skoh): Francis

Goffredo (gohf-FREH-doh): Jeffrey

Giorgio (jee‿OHR-jee‿oh): George

Giuseppe‧(jee‿oo-ZEHP-pay): Joseph

Gregorio (gray-GO-ree‿oh): Gregory

Gualtiero (goo‿ahl-tee‿EH-roh): Walter

Guglielmo (goo-lyee‿EHL-moh): William

Patrizio (pah-TREET-see‿oh): Patrick

Paolo (PAH‿oh-loh): Paul

Raimondo (rah‿ee-MOHN-doh): Raymond

Riccardo (ree-KAHR-doh): Richard

Roberto (roh-BEHR-toh): Robert

Rinaldo (ree-NAHL-doh): Ronald

Ruggiero (rooj-jee‿EH-roh): Roger

Samuele (sah-moo‿EH-lay): Samuel

Ugo (oo-goh): Hugh

Vincenzo (veen-CHEHNT-soh): Vincent

Select club colors:

arancione

bianco

blu

giallo

grigio

marrone

nero

rosa

rosso

verde

vìola

Perhaps you'd like to adopt the colors used in the Italian flag:

Verde, bianco, rosso.

Here's a game that club members will enjoy. The first one to arrive at the center of the circle wins.

Players will need:

1. A button (if more than one person plays, use a button of a different color for each player).
2. Five slips of paper, numbered 1 to 5 in Italian.
3. A box in which to shake the slips of paper.

Then:

1. Draw a number from the box (if more than one person is playing, take turns). If the number is *uno*, move button one space toward the center. If the number is *due*, move two spaces, etc.
2. Follow directions on space in which button lands, such as:

   "Prendere un altro numero." ("Take another number.")

   "Ritornare alla casa." ("Return to the house.")

   "Muovere alla Torre Pendente." ("Move to the Leaning Tower.")
3. Return each slip to the box after each drawing. Then say to the winner:

   "Congratulazioni!"

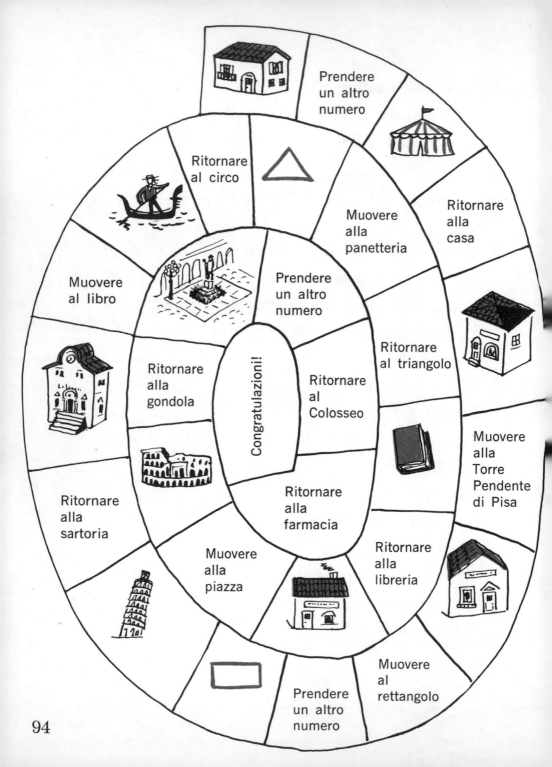

94

Club members will enjoy singing "L'Orso" to the
tune of "The Bear Went Over the Mountain."

L'Orso

L'or - so tra - ver - sa il mon - te, L'or - so tra - ver - sa il
L'al - tro la - to del mon - te, L'al - tro la - to___ del

mon - te, L'or - so tra - ver - sa il mon - te, E
mon - te, L'al - tro la - to___ del mon - te, Ve -

ve - de quel - lo che ve - de, E ve - de quel - lo che
de e ni en - te pi ù. Ve - de e ni en - te

D.C.

ve - de, E ve - de quel - lo che ve - de,
pi ù, Ve - de e ni en - te pi ù,

At Christmas time your club members can sing Christmas carols in Italian. "Santa Notte" is sung to the tune of "Silent Night."

Sante Notte

San - te not - te, Not - te si - len - te; Tut - to è cal - mo,

tut - to è splen - de Ec - co la ver - gi - ne, ma - dre e il bam - bin;

Sa - cro bam - bi - no sì te - ne - ro e bel;

Dor - mi ce - le - ste bam - bin, — Dor - mi ce - le - ste bam - bin.

Here are some other suggested activities for "Il Circolo Italiano":

1. Write to pen-pals in Italy. (Your teacher will be able to secure addresses.)
2. Ask your librarian to plan an "Italian Shelf" in the library.
3. Write for colorful literature on Italy to Italian State Tourist Office, Palazzo d'Italia, Rockefeller Center, 626 Fifth Avenue, New York 20, N.Y. or to Italian Information Center, 686 Park Avenue, New York 21, N.Y.
4. Arrange an Italian Day Assembly for members of your club to sing Italian songs, explain Italian customs, and perhaps act out one of the adventures of Gina and Giovanni.
5. Have a Treasure Hunt! Select some of the objects mentioned in this book, such as a book, pen, pencil, or shoe, and toy animals such as an elephant, monkey, or dog. Hide these objects. Then

let the club members look for them. The one who finds the most and can give their names in Italian wins.

6. Invite parents to a sight-seeing tour of Italy. The tour is taken by means of slides which show interesting views of Italy. Each member can make a comment *in Italian* about a slide.

Arrivederci e buona fortuna, amici!

VOCABOLARIO

Phonetic symbols used:

ah: (*a* in *father*)	j: (*g* in *giraffe*)
ay: (*e* in *hey*)	gh: (*g* in *spaghetti*)
ee: (*ee* in *feet*)	ly: (*ll* in *million*)
eh: (*e* in *net*)	ny: (*ny* in *canyon*)
o: (*o* in *top*)	r: (always rolls)
oh: (*o* in *rope*)	sh: (*sh* in *fish*)
oo: (*oo* in *pool*)	ts: (*ts* in *eats*)
ch: (*ch* in *church*)	
k: (*k* in *key*)	

a (ah): to, at.

addio (ah-DEE‿oh): good-by.

l'aeroplano (ah‿eh-roh-PLAH-noh): airplane.

affettuosamente (ahf-feht-too‿oh-zah-MEHN-tay): affection-
ately.

agosto (ah-GOH-stoh): August.

aiutare (ah-ee‿oo-TAH-ray): to help.

aiuto (ah-ee‿oo-toh): help.

al (ahl): to the (for singular HE word beginning with a
consonant, except *z*, or *s* plus a consonant).

alla (AHL-lah): to the, at the (for singular SHE word).

allo (AHL-loh): to the, at the (for singular HE word beginning with a *z*, or *s* plus a consonant).

allora (ahl-LOH-rah): then.

l'altalena (ahl-tah-LAY-nah): see-saw.

alto: see *in alto.*

altra (AHL-trah): other (for singular SHE word).

altro (AHL-troh): other (for singular HE word).

gli amici (ah-MEE-chee): friends.

ammette (ahm-MEHT-tay): (he, she) admits.

anche (AHN-kay): also.

ancora (ahn-KOH-rah): again, still, more.

andare (ahn-DAH-ray): to go.

gli animali (ah-nee-MAH-lee): animals.

gli anni (AHN-nee): years.

l'antipasto (ahn-tee-PAH-stoh): appetizer.

aprile (ah-PREE-lay): April.

l'aquila (AH-koo ee-lah): eagle.

le aquile (AH-koo ee-lay): eagles.

gli aquilotti (ah-koo ee-LOT-tee): eaglets.

l'aquilotto (ah-koo ee-LOT-toh): eaglet.

arancione (ah-rahn-chee OH-nay): orange (for both HE and SHE words in the singular and plural).

arriva (ahr-REE-vah): (he, she) arrives.

arrivederci (ahr-ree-veh-DEHR-chee): good-by.

gli asparagi (ah-SPAH-rah-jee): asparagus.

le attrazioni (aht-traht-see OH-nee): attractions.

balla (BAHL-lah): (he, she) dances.

ballano (BAHL-lah-noh): (they) dance.

ballare (bahl-LAH-ray): to dance.

la bambina (bahm-BEE-nah): little girl; *il bambino* (bahm-BEE-noh): little boy.

la banda (BAHN-dah): band.

barbuta (bahr-BOO-tah): bearded.

basso: see *in basso.*

becca (BEH-kah): he, she pecks.

bel (behl): beautiful (for singular HE word beginning with a consonant except *z*, or *s* plus a consonant).

bellezza (behl-LAYT-sah): beauty.

belli (BEHL-lee): beautiful (for plural HE word).

bene (BEH-nay): well.

bianca (bee‿AHN-kah): white (for singular SHE word).

bianche (bee‿AHN-kay): white (for plural SHE word).

bianchi (bee‿AHN-kee): white (for plural HE word).

bianco (bee‿AHN-koh): white (for singular HE word).

Bibì (bee-BEE): Bibì.

Bibò (bee-BOH): Bibò.

la bicicletta (bee-chee-KLAYT-tah): bicycle.

i biglietti (bee-lyee‿AYT-tee): tickets.

i birilli (bee-REEL-lee): bowling pins.

il birillo (bee-REEL-loh): bowling pin.

il biscotto (bee-SCOT-toh): cracker.

la bistecca (bee-STAYK-kah): beefsteak.

blu (bloo): blue (for both HE and SHE words in the singular and plural).

la bocca (BOHK-kah): mouth.

la bottiglia (boht-TEE-lyee‿ah): bottle.

bù, bù (boo boo): bow wow.

buffa (BOOF-fah): funny (for singular SHE word).

buon (boo‿ON): good (for singular HE word beginning with a consonant except *z,* or *s* plus a consonant).

buon giorno (boo‿ON jee‿OHR-noh): good day, good morning.

buona (boo‿o-nah): good (for singular SHE word).

buoni (boo‿o-nee): good (for plural HE word).

il caffè (kahf-FEH): coffee.

il calcio (KAHL-chee‿oh): soccer.

il calendario (kah-layn-DAH-ree‿oh): calendar.

calmo (KAHL-moh): calm (for singular HE word).

la camicia (kah-MEE-chee‿ah): shirt.

il cammello (kahm-MEHL-loh): camel.

le candele (kahn-DAY-lay): candles.

il cane (KAH-nay): dog.

i cani (KAH-nee): dogs.

la cangura (kahn-GOO-rah): kangaroo.

canta (KAHN-tah): (he, she) sings.

cantano (KAHN-tah-noh): (they) sing.

capisce (kah-PEE-shay): (he, she) understands.

la capitale (kah-pee-TAH-lay): capital.

il cappello (kahp-PEHL-loh): hat.

la capra (KAH-prah): goat.

caro (KAH-roh): dear (for singular HE word).

le carote (kah-RO-tay): carrots.

il carro (KAHR-roh): cart.

i carri (KAHR-ree): carts.

il cartello (kar-TEHL-loh): sign.

la casa (KAH-sah): house.

c'è (cheh): there is.

celeste (chay-LEH-stay): celestial, heavenly (for singular HE or SHE word).

cento (CHEN-toh): one hundred.

cercate (chayr-KAH-tay): (you [plural]) look for.

i cerchi (CHAYR-kee): circles.

cerchiamo (chayr-kee‿AH-moh): we are looking for, let's look for.

che (kay): who, whom, which, that.

che . . . ! (kay): what a . . . !

chi (kee): who, the one who.

chiamano: see *si chiamano.*

chiamare (kee‿ah-MAH-ray): to call.

la chiave (kee‿AH-vay): key.

chicchirichi (kee-kee-ree-KEE): cock-a-doodle-doo.

chiede (kee‿EH-day): (he, she) asks.

la chioccia (kee‿o-chee‿ah): mother-hen.

la chitarra (kee-TAHR-rah): guitar.

ci (chee): there, here.

ciao (chee‿AH-o): hello, good-by.

la cicogna (chee-KOH-nyah): stork.

cinquanta (cheen-koo‿AHN-tah): fifty.

cinque (CHEEN-koo‿ay): five.

il cioccolato (chee‿oh-koh-LAH-toh): chocolate.

il circo (CHEER-koh): circus.

il circolo (CHEER-koh-loh): club, circle.

la città (cheet-TAH): city.

il ciuco (chee‿oo-koh): donkey.

Cocò (koh-KO): Cocò.

il colore (koh-LOH-ray): color.

il Colosseo (ko-los-SEH-oh): Colosseum.

colpisce (kohl-PEE-shay): (he, she) hits.

colpite (kohl-PEE-tay): hit (command).

come (KOH-may): how, like.

Come stai? (KOH-may STAH‿ee): How are you?

il compleanno (kohm-play-AHN-noh): birthday.

con (kohn): with.

le congratulazioni (kohn-grah-too-laht-see‿o-nee): congratu-
lations.

i conigli (koh-NEE-lyee): rabbits.

il coniglio (koh-NEE-lyee‿oh): rabbit.

conta (KOHN-tah): (he, she) counts.

continua (kohn-TEE-noo‿ah): (he, she) continues.

coraggiosa (koh-rahj-jee‿OH-zah): brave (for singular SHE word).

coraggiosi (koh-rahj-jee‿OH-zee): brave (for plural HE word).

coraggioso (koh-rahj-jee‿OH-zoh): brave (for singular HE word).

la corda (KOHR-dah): rope.

coro: see *in coro.*

corti (KOHR-tee): short (for plural HE word).

la cosa (KOH-sah): thing.

costa (KO-stah): (it) costs.

costano (KOH-stah-noh): (they) cost.

i cuccioli (KOO-chee‿oh-lee): puppies.

il cucciolo (KOO-chee‿oh-loh): puppy.

da (dah): from.

dà (dah): (he, she) gives.

danno (DAHN-noh): (they) give.

dare (DAH-ray): to give.

davanti a (dah-VAHN-tee ah): in front of.

del (dehl): of the (for singular HE word), some.

dell' (dehl): of the (for word beginning with a vowel), some.

della (DEHL-lah): of the (for singular SHE word), some.

il denaro (deh-NAH-roh): money.

di (dee): of, than.

dice (DEE-chay): (he, she) says.

dicembre (dee-CHEHM-bray): December.

dicono (DEE-koh-noh): (they) say.

dieci (dee‿AY-chee): ten.

dietro (dee‿AY-troh): behind.

discende (dee-SHAYN-day): (he, she) descends.

disegna (dee-SAY-nyah): (he, she) draws.

disegnare (dee-say-NYAH-ray): to draw.

il divano (dee-VAH-noh): divan, sofa.

dodici (DOH-dee-chee): twelve.

domanda (doh-MAHN-dah): (he, she) asks.

domandano (doh-MAHN-dah-noh): (they) ask.

la domenica (doh-MAY-nee-kah): Sunday.

la donna (DON-nah): lady, woman.

dormi (DOR-mee): sleep (command).

dove (DOH-vay): where.

dov'è . . . ? (doh-VEH): where is . . . ?

due (DOO_ay): two.

Dumbo (DOOM-boh): Dumbo.

e (ay): and.

è (eh): is; *è l'una* (eh LOO-nah): it is one o'clock.

ecco (EH-koh): here is, here are, there is, there are.

egli (AY-lyee): he.

l'elefante (ay-lay-FAHN-tay): elephant.

gli elefanti (ay-lay-FAHN-tee): elephants.

ella (AYL-lah): she.

enorme (ay-NOR-may): enormous, huge (for singular HE and SHE word).

entrare (ayn-TRAH-ray): to enter.

esclama (ay-SKLAH-mah): (he, she) exclaims.

essere (EHS-say-ray): to be.

essi (AYS-see): they.

fa (fah): (he, she) does, makes.

la faccia (FAH-chee_ah): face.

la fame (FAH-may): hunger; *io ho fame* (EE‿oh oh FAH-
   may): I am hungry.

la famiglia (fah-MEE-lyee‿ah): family.

fare (FAH-ray): to do.

la farmacia (fahr-mah-CHEE‿ah): pharmacy, drugstore.

favore: see *per favore.*

febbraio (fehb-BRAH-ee‿oh): February.

felice (fay-LEE-chay): happy (for singular HE and SHE
   word).

Figaro (FEE-gah-roh): Figaro.

il film (feelm): film.

la fine (FEE-nay): end.

finisce (fee-NEE-shay): (he, she) finishes.

la fontana (fohn-TAH-nah): fountain.

la fortuna (fohr-TOO-nah): fortune, luck.

la fotografia (foh-toh-grah-FEE‿ah): photograph.

fra (frah): among.

il fratello (frah-TEHL-loh): brother.

la frutta (FROOT-tah): fruit.

il gallo (GAHL-loh): rooster.

la gatta (GAHT-tah): cat.

il gelato (jay-LAH-toh): ice cream.

gennaio (jayn-NAH-ee‿oh): January.

getta (JEHT-tah): (he, she) throws.

il ghiaccio (ghee‿AH-chee‿oh): ice.

il ghiro (GHEE-roh): dormouse.

gialli (jee‿AHL-lee): yellow (for plural HE word).

giallo (jee‿AHL-loh): yellow (for singular HE word).

Gina (JEE-nah): Gina.

giocare (jee_oh-KAH-ray): to play.

il giocoliere (jee_oh-koh-lee_EH-ray): juggler.

i giorni (jee_OHR-nee): days.

il giorno (jee_OHR-noh): day; *buon giorno* (boo_ON jee_OHR-noh): good day, good morning.

Giovanni (jee_oh-VAHN-nee): John.

giovedì (jee_oh-vay-DEE): Thursday.

gira (JEE-rah): (he, she) turns.

la giraffa (jee-RAHF-fah): giraffe.

le giraffe (jee-RAHF-fay): giraffes.

girare (jee-RAH-ray): to spin around.

giù (jee_oo): down.

giugno (jee_oo-nyoh): June.

gli (lyee): the (before plural HE words beginning with a vowel, or *z*, or *s* plus a consonant).

la gondola (GOHN-doh-lah): gondola.

grande (GRAHN-day): big, great (for singular HE or SHE word).

grandi (GRAHN-dee): big, great (for plural HE or SHE word).

la grassona (grahs-SOH-nah): fat lady.

grazie (GRAHT-see_ay): thank you.

grida (GREE-dah): (he, she) shouts.

grigio (GREE-jee_oh): gray (for singular HE word).

grossa (GROS-sah): large (for singular SHE word).

grossi (GROS-see): large (for plural HE word).

grosso (GROS-soh): large (for singular HE word).

guarda (goo_AHR-dah): (he, she) looks, looks at.

guarda! (goo_AHR-dah): look!, look at . . .

guardano (goo_AHR-dah-noh): (they) look, look at.

guardare (goo_ahr-DAH-ray): to look, look at.

ha (ah): (he, she) has.

hai (AH‿ee): (you) have.

hanno (AHN-noh): (they) have.

ho (o): (I) have.

i (ee): the (before plural HE words beginning with a consonant except *z*, or *s* plus a consonant).

l'idea (ee-DAY-ah): idea.

il (eel): the (before singular HE words beginning with a consonant except *z*, or *s* with a consonant).

imita (EE-mee-tah): (he, she) imitates.

in (een): in.

in alto (een AHL-toh): up.

in basso (een BAHS-soh): down.

in coro (een KO-roh): all together.

gli indiani (een-dee‿AH-nee): Indians.

indice (EEN-dee-chay): table of contents.

l'insalata (een-sah-LAH-tah): salad.

inseguono (een-SAY-goo‿oh-noh): (they) follow.

intelligente (een-tehl-lee-JEHN-tay): intelligent (for singular HE or SHE word).

interessante (een-tay-rehs-SAHN-tay): interesting (for singular HE or SHE word).

intorno a (een-TOHR-noh ah): around.

io (EE‿oh): I.

l'ippopotamo (eep-poh-PO-tah-moh): hippopotamus.

Italia (ee-TAH-lee‿ah): Italy.

italiano (ee-tah-lee‿AH-noh): Italian (for singular HE word).

l': the (before singular HE or SHE words beginning with a vowel).

la (lah): the (before singular SHE words beginning with a consonant).

là (lah): there.

la lancetta (lahn-CHEHT-tah): clock or watch hand.

lascia (LAH-shee‿ah): (he, she) leaves.

lasciare (lah-shee‿AH-ray): to leave.

il lato (LAH-toh): side.

il latte (LAHT-tay): milk.

le (lay): the (before all plural SHE words).

legge (LEHJ-jay): (he, she) reads.

leggere l'ora (LEHJ-jeh-ray LOH-rah): to tell time.

leggono (LEHG-goh-noh): (they) read.

il leone (lay-OH-nay): lion.

i leoni (lay-OH-nee): lions.

la lettera (LEHT-tay-rah): letter.

la libreria (lee-bray-REE‿ah): bookstore.

il libro (LEE-broh): book.

la limonata (lee-moh-NAH-tah): lemonade.

la lira (LEE-rah): an Italian coin.

le lire (LEE-ray): Italian coins.

la lista (LEE-stah): menu.

lo (loh): the (before singular HE words beginning with *z,* or *s* plus a consonant).

luglio (LOO-lyee‿oh): July.

lunedì (loo-nay-DEE): Monday.

lunghe (LOON-ghay): long (for plural SHE word).

lunghi (LOON-ghee): long (for plural HE word).

ma (mah): but.

la madre (MAH-dray): mother.

maggio (MAJ-jce‿oh): May.

magnifica (mah-NYEE-fee-kah): magnificent (for singular SHE word).

il mago (MAH-goh): magician.

la mamma (MAHM-mah): mama; *mamma mia!* (mahm-mah MEE_ah): dear me!

manda (MAHN-dah): (he, she) sends, send (command).

mangia (MAHN-jee_ah): (he, she) eats, eat (command).

mangiano (MAHN-jee_ah-noh): (they) eat.

mangiare (mahn-jee_AH-ray): to eat.

le mani (MAH-nee): hands.

Marco (MAHR-koh): Mark.

Maria (mah-REE_ah): Mary.

marrone (mahr-ROH-nay): brown (for singular word).

martedì (mahr-tay-DEE): Tuesday.

marzo (MAHRT-soh): March.

la matita (mah-TEE-tah): pencil.

meraviglioso (may-rah-vee-lyee_OH-zoh): marvelous (for singular HE word).

mercoledì (mehr-coh-lay-DEE): Wednesday.

il mese (MAY-zay): month.

mette (MEHT-tay): (he, she) puts.

mezza (MEHD-zah): half (for singular SHE word).

mi (mee): me, to me.

mia (MEE-ah): mine, my (for singular SHE word).

miei (mee_AY_ee): mine, my (for plural HE word).

mio (MEE-oh): mine, my (for singular HE word).

molta (MOHL-tah): much, many (for singular SHE word).

molte (MOHL-tay): much, many (for plural SHE word).

molti (MOHL-tee): many (for plural HE word).

molto (MOHL-toh): very.

il mondo (MOHN-doh): world.

110

la moneta (moh-NAY-tah): coin.

il monte (MOHN-tay): mountain.

la mozzarella (mot-sah-REHL-lah): mozzarella cheese.

muove (moo‿o-vay): (he, she) moves.

muovere (moo‿o-veh-ray): to move.

la musica (MOO-zee-kah): music.

il naso (NAH-zoh): nose.

naturalmente (nah-too-rahl-MAYN-tay): naturally.

nel (nehl): in the (for singular HE word beginning with
        a consonant, except *z*, or *s* plus a consonant).

nella (NEHL-lah): in the (for singular SHE word).

nelle (NEHL-lay): in the (for plural SHE word).

nera (NAY-rah): black (for singular SHE word).

nere (NAY-ray): black (for plural SHE word).

neri (NAY-ree): black (for plural HE word).

nero (NAY-roh): black (for singular HE word).

niente (nee‿EHN-tay): nothing.

no (no): no.

noi (NOH‿ee): we.

non (nohn): not.

la notte (NOT-tay): night.

novanta (noh-VAHN-tah): ninety.

nove (NO-vay): nine.

novembre (noh-VEHM-bray): November.

il numero (NOO-may-roh): number.

la nuvola (NOO-voh-lah): cloud.

le nuvole (NOO-voh-lay): clouds.

l'occhio (o-kee‿oh): eye.

oggi (OJ-jee): today.

l'ombra (OHM-brah): shadow.

l'ora (OH-rah): time.

le orecchie (o-REH-kee_ay): ears.

l'orologio (oh-roh-LO-jee_oh): clock.

gli orsi (OHR-see): bears.

l'orso (OHR-soh): bear.

ottanta (oht-TAHN-tah): eighty.

otto (OT-toh): eight.

ottobre (oht-TOH-bray): October.

il padre (PAH-dray): father.

la pagina (PAH-jee-nah): page.

il pagliaccio (pah-lyee_AH-chee_oh): clown.

il palazzo (pah-LAHT-soh): palace.

la palla (PAHL-lah): ball.

le palle (PAHL-lay): balls.

il pallone (pahl-LOH-nay): balloon.

i palloni (pahl-LOH-nee): balloons.

la panetteria (pah-neht-tay-REE_ah): bakery.

i pantaloni (pahn-tah-LOH-nee): trousers.

il pappagallo (pahp-pah-GAHL-loh): parrot.

parlante (pahr-LAHN-tay): talking.

partire (pahr-TEE-ray): to leave.

passa (PAHS-sah): (he, she) passes.

passano (PAHS-sah-noh): (they) pass.

pattina (PAHT-tee-nah): (he, she) skates.

la paura (pah_oo-rah): fear; *ha paura* (ah pah_oo-rah): (he, she) is afraid.

pendente (pehn-DEHN-tay): leaning.

la penna (PAYN-nah): pen.

per (pehr.): for, through.

per favore (pehr fah-VOH-ray): please.

perchè (pehr-KAY): because, why.

la persona (pehr-SOH-nah): person.

pesante (pay-SAHN-tay): heavy.

il pesce (PAY-shay): fish.

piange (pee‿AHN-jay): (he, she) cries.

la piazza (pee‿AHT-sah): public square.

piccola (PEEK-koh-lah): small (for singular SHE word).

piccoli (PEEK-koh-lee): small (for plural HE word).

piccolo (PEEK-koh-loh): small (for singular HE word).

pilotare (pee-loh-TAH-ray): to pilot.

il pinguino (peen-goo‿EE-noh): penguin.

Pisa (PEE-sah): Pisa.

più (pee‿oo): more, any longer.

la pizza (PEET-sah): pizza pie.

poco (PO-koh): little, small amount.

Pogo (PO-goh): Pogo.

poi (PO‿ee): then, afterwards.

porta (POR-tah): (he, she) carries, brings, wears.

portano (POR-tah-noh): (they) carry, bring, wear.

possibile (pohs-SEE-bee-lay): possible.

povera (PO-vay-rah): poor (for singular SHE word).

preferito (pray-fay-REE-toh): preferred (for singular HE word).

prego (PREH-goh): you're welcome.

prende (PREHN-day): (he, she) takes.

prendere (PREHN-day-ray): to take.

il presidente (preh-see-DEHN-tay): president (HE).

la presidentessa (preh-see-dehn-TEHS-sah): president (SHE).

presto (PREH-stoh): soon, early.

il programma (proh-GRAHM-mah): program.

prossima (PROS-see-mah): next (for singular SHE word).

pum! (poom): bang!

la punta (POON-tah): point.

le punte (POON-tay): points.

il quadrato (koo‿ah-DRAH-toh): square.

qualche (koo‿AHL-kay): some.

qualche cosa (koo‿AHL-kay KOH-sah): something.

quale (koo‿AH-lay): which (for singular HE or SHE word).

quando (koo‿AHN-doh): when.

quanti (koo‿AHN-tee): how many (for plural HE word).

quanto (koo‿AHN-toh): how much (for singular HE word).

quaranta (koo‿ah-RAHN-tah): forty.

quattro (koo‿AHT-troh): four.

quello (koo‿AYL-loh): that; *quello che* (koo‿AYL-loh kay):
    that which, what.

questa (koo‿AY-stah): *questo* (koo‿AY-stoh): this.

queste (koo‿AY-stay): these.

qui (koo‿EE): here.

quieti (koo‿ee‿EH-tee): quiet (for plural HE word).

quieto (koo‿ee‿EH-toh): quiet (for singular HE word).

quindici (koo‿EEN-dee-chee): fifteen.

la ragazza (rah-GAHT-sah): girl.

le ragazze (rah-GAHT-say): girls.

i ragazzi (rah-GAHT-see): boys.

il ragazzo (rah-GAHT-soh): boy.

i ravioli (rah-vee‿OH-lee): ravioli.

i regali (ray-GAH-lee): presents.

il regalo (ray-GAH-loh): present.

il resto (REH-stoh): rest, remainder.

il rettangolo (reht-TAHN-goh-loh): rectangle.

riappare (ree_ahp-PAH-ray): (he, she) reappears.

risponde (ree-SPOHN-day): (he, she) answers.

rispondono (ree-SPOHN-doh-noh): (they) answer.

il ristorante (ree-stoh-RAHN-tay): restaurant.

ritorna (ree-TOHR-nah): (he, she) returns.

ritornano (ree-TOHR-nah-noh): (they) return.

ritornare (ree-tohr-NAH-ray): to return.

rosa (RO-zah): pink (for both HE and SHE words in the
    singular and plural).

rossa (ROHS-sah): red (for singular SHE word).

rossi (ROHS-see): red (for plural HE word).

rosso (ROHS-soh): red (for singular HE word).

rotola (RO-toh-lah): (he, she) rolls.

sa (sah): (he, she) knows, knows how to.

sabato (SAH-bah-toh): Saturday.

sacro (SAH-kroh): sacred, holy (for singular HE word).

sai (SAH_ee): (you) know, know how to

sale (SAH-lay): (he, she) goes up.

salire (sah-LEE-ray): to go up.

salta (SAHL-tah): (he, she) jumps over.

saltare (sahl-TAH-ray): to jump over.

sanno (SAHN-noh): (they) know, know how to.

santa (SAHN-tah): holy (for singular SHE word).

sappiamo (sahp-pee_AH-moh): (we) know, know how to.

la sartoria (sahr-toh-REE_ah): tailor shop.

le scale (SKAH-lay): stairs.

la scarpa (SKAHR-pah): shoe.

la scatola (SKAH-toh-lah): box.

la scimmia (SHEEM-mee_ah): monkey.

le scimmie (SHEEM-mee‿ay): monkeys.

lo scimpanzè (sheem-pahnt-SAY): chimpanzee.

lo scoiattolo (skoh-ee‿AHT-toh-loh): squirrel.

scompare (skohm-PAH-ray): (he, she) disappears.

scomparire (skohm-pah-REE-ray): to disappear.

scoppiano (SKOP-pee‿ah-noh): (they) burst.

scritto (SKREET-toh): written.

scrive (SKREE-vay): (he, she) writes.

scrivo (SKREE-voh): (I) write.

scrivono (SKREE-voh-noh): (they) write.

la sedia (SEH-dee‿ah): chair.

seduto (seh-DOO-toh): seated.

la segretaria (seh-gray-TAH-ree‿ah): secretary (SHE).

il segretario (seh-gray-TAH-ree‿oh): secretary (HE).

sei (SEH‿ee): six.

sempre (SEHM-pray): always.

il serpente (sehr-PEHN-tay): serpent.

sessanta (sehs-SAHN-tah): sixty.

settanta (seht-TAHN-tah): seventy.

sette (SEHT-tay): seven.

settembre (seht-TEHM-bray): September.

la settimana (seht-tee-MAH-nah): week.

si (see): themselves; *si chiamano* (see kee‿AH-mah-noh): they are called.

sì (see): yes, so.

la signora (see-NYO-rah): the woman.

il signore (see-NYO-ray): the man.

silente (see-LAYN-tay): silent (for singular HE or SHE word).

lo smilzo (SMEELT-soh): thin man.

so (so): (I) know, know how to.

sogna (soh-nyah): (he, she) dreams.

solamente (soh-lah-MEHN-tay): only.

il sole (soh-lay): sun.

solleva (sohl-LAY-vah): (he, she) raises.

sono (soh-noh): they are, I am.

sono le due (soh-noh lay DOO_ay): it is two o'clock.

la sorella (soh-REHL-lah): sister.

sorride (sohr-REE-day): (he, she) smiles.

sotto (soHT-toh): under.

gli spaghetti (spah-GHEHT-tee): spaghetti.

gli spinaci (spee-NAH-chee): spinach.

splende (SPLEHN-day): (he, she) shines.

sta (stah): (he, she) is.

stai (STAH_ee): (you) are.

stanno (STAHN-noh): (they) are.

sto (sto): I am.

su (soo): on, up.

sua (soo_ah): her, hers, his (for singular SHE word).

sue (soo_ay): her, hers, his (for plural SHE word).

suo (soo_oh): her, hers, his (for singular HE word).

suoi (soo_o_ee): her, hers, his (for plural HE word).

sull' (sool): on the (for singular HE word beginning with
     a vowel).

sulla (sooL-lah): on the (for singular SHE word beginning
     with a consonant).

suona (soo_o-nah): (he, she) plays; *suona la chitarra*
     (soo_o-nah lah kee-TAHR-rah): he, she plays the
     guitar.

il tavolo (TAH-voh-loh): table.

te (teh): you, to you.

la televisione (teh-leh-vee-see‿OH-nay): television.

teme (TAY-may): (he, she) fears.

tenero (TAY-nay-roh): tender (for singular HE word).

la terra (TEHR-rah): earth.

la tesoriera (tay-soh-ree‿EH-rah): treasurer (SHE).

il tesoriere (tay-soh-ree‿EH-ray): treasurer (HE).

la testa (TEH-stah): head.

Titta (TEET-tah): Titta.

la tombola (TOHM-boh-lah): bingo.

Tonio (TO-nee‿oh): Tony.

la torre (TOHR-ray): tower.

la Torre Pendente di Pisa (TOHR-ray pehn-DEHN-tay dee PEE-sah): leaning tower of Pisa.

la torta (TOHR-tah): cake.

traversa (trah-VEHR-sah): (he, she) crosses.

tre (tray): three.

trenta (TRAYN-tah): thirty.

Trevi (TRAY-vee): Trevi.

il triangolo (tree‿AHN-goh-loh): triangle.

triste (TREE-stay): sad (for singular HE or SHE word).

trova (TRO-vah): (he, she) finds.

trovano (TRO-vah-noh): (they) find.

tu (too): you.

tuo (TOO‿oh): your, yours (for singular HE word).

tuoi (too‿o‿ee): your, yours (for plural HE word).

tutto (TOOT-toh): all (for singular HE word).

tutti (TOOT-tee): all (for plural HE word).

un (oon): a, an, one (before most HE words).

un' (oon): a, an; one (before a SHE word beginning with a vowel).

una (oo-nah): a, an, one (before singular SHE word beginning with a consonant).

undici (OON-dee-chee): eleven.

uno (oo-noh): a, an, one (before HE word beginning with *z,* or *s* plus a consonant).

l'uomo (oo‿o-moh): man.

vanno (VAHN-noh): (they) go.

la vasca (VAH-skah): pool.

vede (VAY-day): (he, she) sees.

vedere (vay-DAY-ray): to see.

vedono (VAY-doh-noh): (they) see.

venerdì (vay-nayr-DEE): Friday.

venire (vay-NEE-ray): to come.

venti (VAYN-tee): twenty.

verde (VAYR-day): green (for singular HE or SHE word).

verdi (VAYR-dee): green (for plural HE or SHE word).

la vergine (VAYR-jee-nay): virgin.

vero (VAY-roh): true (for singular HE word).

il vice-presidente (VEE-chay preh-see-DEHN-tay): vice president (HE).

la vice-presidentessa (VEE-chay preh-see-dehn-TEHS-sah): vice president (SHE).

viene (vee‿EH-nay): (he, she) comes.

vince (VEEN-chay): (he, she) wins.

vincere (VEEN-chay-ray): to win.

vincete (veen-CHAY-tay): win (command).

viòla (vee‿o-lah): purple (for both HE and SHE words in the singular and plural).

visto (VEE-stoh): seen.

il vocabolario (voh-kah-boh-LAH-ree‿oh): vocabulary.

vogliamo (voh-lyee‿AH-moh): (we) want.

voglio (vo-lyee‿oh): (I) want.

vogliono (vo-lee‿oh-noh): (they) want.

voi (VOH‿ee): you (plural).

vola (VOH-lah): (he, she) flies.

la volta (VOL-tah): time.

vuoi (voo‿o‿ee): (you) want; *vuoi . . . ?* (voo‿o‿ee):
    do you want?

vuole (voo‿o-lay): (he, she) wants.

la zebra (DZAY-brah): zebra.

la zia (TSEE‿ah): aunt.

lo zio (TSEE‿oh): uncle.